Challenges in IT and Digital Marketing

C. P. Kumar
Reiki Healer & Author
Roorkee - 247667, India

Disclaimer

While every effort has been made to ensure the accuracy and completeness of the content in this book, the author cannot guarantee that the information contained herein is error-free, up-to-date, or suitable for every individual circumstance.

The author shall not be held liable or responsible for any errors or omissions in the content of the book, nor for any damages, or losses that may arise from any actions taken based upon the suggestions or contents presented in the book.

Readers are advised to use their own judgment and discretion in applying the information provided in this book, and to consult with qualified professionals before taking any action based on the contents of this book. The author disclaims any and all liability or responsibility for any actions taken or not taken based on the information contained in this book.

DEDICATION

This book is dedicated to the resilient and forward-thinking professionals in the realms of Information Technology and Digital Marketing. To those who navigate the ever-changing technological terrain with unwavering determination, embracing the challenges posed by rapid advancements.

To the perpetual learners committed to continuous education, ensuring their relevance in a dynamic field where obsolescence looms. To the guardians of the digital realm, who tirelessly combat cyber threats and safeguard data in an era of escalating challenges.

To the compliance navigators, who deftly maneuver through regulatory frameworks, ensuring adherence to strict data protection and privacy requirements. To the communicators bridging the gap between technical intricacies and the broader organizational landscape, fostering collaboration and understanding.

To the strategic aligners of IT and business goals, creating a symbiotic relationship that drives mutual success. To the project managers facing scope changes, tight timelines, and project clock races with resilience and integrity.

To the digital marketers navigating algorithmic adventures, data privacy dilemmas, and the complexities of real-time engagement, rising above the noise in a saturated digital landscape. To the analysts and measurers of ROI, decoding digital data and attributing conversions in the intricate world of marketing campaigns.

To the global strategists adapting to diverse cultural contexts and markets, and to the seekers and cultivators of digital talent, bridging the skills gap in a competitive job market. To those facing budget blues, maximizing ROI in digital marketing campaigns despite financial constraints.

May this dedication be a testament to the collective efforts of these professionals - the unsung heroes shaping the future of technology and marketing with resilience, creativity, and an unwavering commitment to overcoming challenges.

C. P. Kumar

CONTENTS

PREFACE

In the ever-evolving landscape of Information Technology (IT) and Digital Marketing, professionals find themselves navigating a dynamic and challenging terrain. This book "Challenges in IT and Digital Marketing" embarks on a comprehensive exploration of the multifaceted challenges encountered by IT and digital marketing practitioners in the contemporary digital age. As technology advances at an unprecedented pace, so too do the hurdles that IT professionals face in maintaining relevance and proficiency.

The opening chapter sets the stage by delving into "*The Ever-Changing Technological Terrain*". We examine the rapid strides in technology, recognizing the perpetual struggle IT professionals face in keeping abreast of the latest trends. From artificial intelligence to blockchain, the relentless progression of technology requires a constant commitment to learning and adaptation.

Moving forward, we address the critical importance of ongoing education in "*Navigating Obsolescence*". This chapter underscores the necessity for IT professionals to continually hone their skills to stay relevant in a field where obsolescence is a constant threat.

The digital realm, while offering boundless opportunities, also poses significant risks, especially in terms of cybersecurity. "*Guardians of the Digital Realm*" uncovers the escalating threats of cyberattacks and the tireless efforts required to safeguard precious data and systems.

Regulatory compliance is another formidable challenge explored in *"Compliance Tightrope"*. We unravel the complexities faced by IT professionals in adhering to stringent regulatory frameworks, especially in industries with heightened data protection and privacy requirements.

Communication breakdowns between IT professionals and non-technical stakeholders are addressed in *"Interdepartmental Jargon"*. Effective collaboration is underscored as a necessity for successful project execution.

The intricate dance between IT and business goals takes center stage in *"IT and Business Alignment"*. Here, we explore methods to align IT initiatives with overall business objectives, fostering a more symbiotic relationship.

As we delve into the world of digital marketing, the challenges become equally complex. *"Algorithmic Adventures"* unveils the impact of frequent algorithm updates on digital marketing strategies, while *"Data Privacy Dilemmas in the Digital Age"* scrutinizes the challenges marketers face in maintaining data privacy compliance.

"Content Overload" confronts the modern dilemma of creating and promoting engaging content in a saturated digital landscape, and *"Real-Time Engagement"* explores the pressures of meeting consumer expectations for instant responses across digital channels.

The latter half of the book navigates through the intricacies of digital marketing, from decoding digital data and measuring ROI in *"Decoding Digital Data"* to addressing the challenges of tailoring marketing for diverse audiences in *"Globalization Hurdles"*.

The book concludes with a reflection on the human element of these professions. "*Digital Talent Wars*" and "*Budget Blues*" explore the challenges of acquiring and retaining skilled professionals and demonstrating campaign effectiveness amidst budget constraints.

As we embark on this journey through the challenges of IT and digital marketing, we invite readers to explore the solutions, strategies, and insights presented within these pages. The digital age may pose challenges, but within these challenges lie opportunities for growth, innovation, and professional excellence.

C. P. Kumar
Reiki Healer & Author
Former Scientist 'G', National Institute of Hydrology
Roorkee - 247667, India
Web: https://www.angelfire.com/nh/cpkumar/virgo.html

Introduction

In the fast-paced realm of Information Technology (IT) and Digital Marketing, the only constant is change. The landscape of technology is in a perpetual state of flux, evolving at an unprecedented rate. As we delve into the first chapter of our exploration into the Challenges in IT and Digital Marketing, it's crucial to understand and appreciate the dynamism that characterizes the ever-changing technological terrain.

The Acceleration of Technological Advancements

The last few decades have witnessed a technological revolution that has transformed the way we live, work, and interact. From the advent of personal computers to the rise of the internet and the proliferation of smartphones, technology has become an integral part of our daily lives. However, what sets this era apart is the accelerating pace of technological advancements.

The concept of Moore's Law, which posits that the processing power of computers doubles approximately every two years, has held true for several decades. This relentless pace of improvement has given rise to breakthroughs in artificial intelligence, machine learning, blockchain, and the Internet of Things (IoT). As a result, IT professionals find themselves on a perpetual treadmill, constantly striving to stay abreast of the latest developments.

The Challenges of Keeping Pace

For IT professionals, the challenge lies not only in understanding the latest technologies but also in adapting their skill sets to remain relevant. The skills that were in vogue just a few years ago may now be obsolete, replaced by newer, more advanced capabilities. This necessitates a continuous process of learning and upskilling, placing a considerable burden on individuals and organizations alike.

One significant challenge stems from the sheer volume of information available. With the internet serving as a vast repository of knowledge, IT professionals must sift through an ever-expanding sea of information to identify what is relevant and valuable. The ability to discern signal from noise becomes a critical skill, as the sheer volume of data can be overwhelming.

Moreover, the financial implications of constant upskilling cannot be ignored. Training programs, certifications, and courses come with a cost, both in terms of time and money. Small and medium-sized enterprises, in particular, may find it challenging to allocate resources for continuous training, potentially leading to a skills gap within the workforce.

Adaptability as a Core Competency

In the face of these challenges, adaptability emerges as a core competency for IT professionals. The ability to quickly grasp new concepts, languages, and frameworks is no longer a luxury but a necessity. Professionals who can navigate the ever-changing technological landscape with agility are the ones who will thrive in this dynamic environment.

Adaptability extends beyond individual skill sets to organizational structures and cultures. Companies that foster a culture of innovation and continuous learning are better positioned to navigate the challenges posed by the rapid pace of technological change. This involves creating an environment where employees are encouraged to experiment, take risks, and embrace change rather than resist it.

The Evolution of Digital Marketing

The impact of rapid technological advancements is not limited to the IT sector alone; it permeates every facet of the digital landscape, including marketing. Digital Marketing, once a relatively straightforward endeavor, has undergone a radical transformation in recent years.

The proliferation of data analytics tools, coupled with the advent of artificial intelligence, has enabled marketers to delve into the psyche of consumers with unprecedented depth. Personalized marketing, targeted advertising, and predictive analytics are no longer futuristic concepts but integral components of a successful digital marketing strategy.

However, this evolution comes with its own set of challenges. The same technological advancements that empower marketers also present ethical dilemmas and privacy concerns. Striking the right balance between leveraging data for personalized marketing and respecting user privacy has become a delicate tightrope walk.

Privacy Concerns and Ethical Considerations

As digital marketing becomes increasingly sophisticated, the collection and utilization of user data have come under intense scrutiny. High-profile data breaches and scandals have eroded public trust in the way companies handle personal information. This places an additional burden on digital marketers to operate transparently and ethically.

The General Data Protection Regulation (GDPR) in Europe and similar regulations worldwide underscore the need for a more responsible approach to data usage. Marketers must navigate a complex web of regulations and legal considerations to ensure compliance, adding a layer of complexity to their already challenging roles.

Conclusion

The ever-changing technological terrain presents both opportunities and challenges for IT professionals and digital marketers alike. The pace of change is unlikely to decelerate, and as we venture further into the digital age, the ability to adapt and innovate will be paramount.

This chapter serves as a foundational exploration into the multifaceted challenges that define the landscape of IT and Digital Marketing. As we progress through this book, we will delve deeper into specific challenges, strategies for overcoming them, and the future trajectory of these dynamic fields. In the face of the relentless march of technology, the journey promises to be both exhilarating and demanding, requiring a resilient spirit and a commitment to continuous learning and evolution.

Introduction

In the ever-evolving landscape of Information Technology (IT) and Digital Marketing, the only constant is change. As technologies advance at an unprecedented pace, IT professionals find themselves in a perpetual race against obsolescence. This article explores the critical importance of continuous learning in IT and the skills that professionals must cultivate to remain relevant in this dynamic field.

The Rapid Evolution of Technology

The IT industry is marked by rapid and continuous advancements. From artificial intelligence to blockchain, the speed of innovation is both thrilling and challenging. As new technologies emerge, older ones become obsolete, creating a constant need for IT professionals to adapt and stay ahead. This phenomenon has given rise to the concept of continuous learning as a cornerstone for success in the IT realm.

The Importance of Continuous Learning

1. Adaptability as a Survival Skill

In the IT sector, adaptability is not merely a desirable trait; it is a survival skill. Professionals who fail to keep pace with emerging technologies risk falling behind and, ultimately, becoming obsolete. Continuous learning is the bridge that allows IT experts to traverse the ever-widening gap between what they know and what they need to know.

2. Staying Ahead in the Digital Arms Race

The IT landscape can be likened to a digital arms race where staying ahead of the competition is contingent upon acquiring and mastering new skills. Continuous learning ensures that IT professionals are not just keeping up but leading the charge, enabling organizations to harness the power of cutting-edge technologies for a competitive edge.

3. Enhancing Problem-Solving Skills

Continuous learning sharpens an IT professional's problem-solving skills. As they encounter new challenges posed by evolving technologies, the ability to troubleshoot and devise innovative solutions becomes paramount. This not only ensures personal growth but contributes significantly to the efficiency and effectiveness of the organizations they serve.

The Evolving Skill Set

1. Programming Languages and Frameworks

One of the foundational aspects of IT is programming. As new programming languages and frameworks emerge, IT professionals must adapt and become proficient in these tools. Whether it's Python, JavaScript, or a new framework like React or Angular, staying current is non-negotiable.

2. Cloud Computing Mastery

The shift to cloud computing has revolutionized IT infrastructure. Professionals need to continually deepen their understanding of cloud services, such as AWS, Azure, and Google Cloud. The ability to navigate and optimize cloud environments is critical for scalability, security, and overall system efficiency.

3. Data Science and Analytics

In an era dominated by big data, data science and analytics have become integral components of IT. Proficiency in tools like Apache Hadoop, Spark, and machine learning algorithms is essential for extracting meaningful insights from vast datasets. Continuous learning in this domain is crucial for leveraging data as a strategic asset.

4. Cybersecurity Vigilance

With the proliferation of cyber threats, cybersecurity is a top priority for organizations. IT professionals must stay abreast of the latest security protocols, tools, and threat landscapes. Continuous learning in cybersecurity is not only about defense but also understanding the evolving tactics of cyber adversaries.

5. User Experience (UX) Design

As digital interfaces become more prevalent, the importance of UX design cannot be overstated. IT professionals need to grasp the principles of user-centered design, accessibility, and the latest UX trends. Continuous learning in UX ensures that technology remains user-friendly and aligns with evolving user expectations.

Challenges in Continuous Learning

1. Time Constraints

Continuous learning requires an investment of time, a precious commodity for busy IT professionals. Balancing work responsibilities with the need for ongoing education can be challenging, requiring effective time management and prioritization.

2. Resource Accessibility

Access to quality learning resources is crucial for continuous learning. However, not all professionals have equal access to training materials, courses, or mentorship opportunities. Bridging this resource gap is essential for creating an inclusive learning environment in the IT industry.

3. Overcoming Resistance to Change

Some IT professionals may resist continuous learning due to a fear of change or a comfort with existing skills. Overcoming this resistance requires a cultural shift within organizations, emphasizing the benefits of ongoing education for personal and collective success.

Strategies for Effective Continuous Learning

1. Structured Learning Paths

Establishing structured learning paths, whether through formal education or self-paced online courses, provides IT professionals with a clear roadmap for skill development. This approach helps individuals stay focused on acquiring the specific skills needed for their career goals.

2. Collaborative Learning Communities

Creating or participating in collaborative learning communities fosters knowledge exchange among IT professionals. Forums, online groups, and mentorship programs facilitate the sharing of experiences, insights, and best practices, enriching the learning experience.

3. Hands-On Projects and Real-world Applications

Learning by doing is a powerful approach. IT professionals should engage in hands-on projects and real-world applications of new technologies. This not only reinforces theoretical knowledge but also enhances practical problem-solving skills.

4. Regular Skills Assessment

Regular skills assessments are essential for gauging proficiency and identifying areas for improvement. Whether through certifications, online quizzes, or practical exams, these assessments provide tangible benchmarks for measuring continuous learning progress.

Conclusion

Continuous learning is not a choice but a necessity in the dynamic field of IT and Digital Marketing. Embracing a mindset of perpetual growth and adaptation is the key to navigating obsolescence. By prioritizing ongoing education and staying abreast of evolving technologies, IT professionals can not only survive but thrive in an era of rapid technological advancement. As the digital landscape continues to reshape itself, the commitment to continuous learning remains the linchpin for success in the ever-evolving world of IT.

Introduction

In the rapidly evolving landscape of IT and digital marketing, the role of cybersecurity has become paramount. As businesses and individuals alike rely more heavily on digital platforms, the threats posed by cyberattacks have escalated exponentially. In this article, we will delve into the intricate challenges faced by IT professionals in safeguarding the digital realm, exploring the evolving nature of cyber threats and the constant battle to protect sensitive data and systems.

The Evolving Landscape of Cyber Threats

The digital age has brought unprecedented opportunities for connectivity and innovation, but it has also opened the floodgates to a myriad of cyber threats. From traditional malware and phishing attacks to more sophisticated ransomware and zero-day exploits, the arsenal of cybercriminals continues to expand. The evolution of threats necessitates a dynamic and adaptive approach to cybersecurity.

1. Rise of Ransomware Attacks

One of the most prominent and financially motivated cyber threats in recent years has been the surge in ransomware attacks. Cybercriminals employ advanced encryption techniques to lock down critical data, demanding ransoms in cryptocurrency for its release. These attacks not only disrupt business operations but also pose significant financial risks, making them a top concern for IT professionals.

2. Sophistication of Phishing Techniques

Phishing attacks have evolved from crude email scams to highly sophisticated social engineering tactics. Cybercriminals exploit psychological vulnerabilities, using deceptive emails, fake websites, and malicious links to trick users into divulging sensitive information. IT professionals face the challenge of staying one step ahead in the cat-and-mouse game of phishing.

Data Breaches and Privacy Concerns

As businesses accumulate vast amounts of sensitive data, the stakes of a data breach are higher than ever. The fallout from a breach goes beyond financial losses, encompassing damage to reputation, loss of customer trust, and legal ramifications. Safeguarding personal and business data has become a moral imperative, with IT professionals at the forefront of the battle against unauthorized access.

1. Regulatory Compliance and Legal Implications

The regulatory landscape surrounding data protection has become increasingly stringent. Laws such as the General Data Protection Regulation (GDPR) impose strict requirements on organizations to ensure the privacy and security of personal data. Non-compliance not only exposes businesses to financial penalties but also tarnishes their reputation. IT professionals must navigate this complex regulatory environment to avoid legal pitfalls.

2. Protecting Customer Trust

In an era where trust is a fragile commodity, maintaining the confidence of customers is crucial. A single data breach can erode years of hard-earned trust, leading to customer churn and reputational damage. IT professionals play a vital role in implementing robust security measures to safeguard customer data and demonstrate a commitment to privacy and security.

The Human Element: Training and Awareness

While technological solutions are integral to cybersecurity, the human element remains a significant vulnerability. Cybercriminals often exploit human weaknesses through social engineering tactics. In response, IT professionals must prioritize cybersecurity training and awareness programs to empower employees with the knowledge and skills needed to recognize and thwart potential threats.

1. Continuous Training Programs

Cyber threats are dynamic, and so too must be the knowledge of those tasked with defending against them. Continuous training programs are essential to keep IT professionals abreast of the latest attack vectors, trends, and mitigation strategies. Investing in the education and skill development of the cybersecurity workforce is a proactive measure to stay ahead of evolving threats.

2. Fostering a Culture of Cybersecurity

Building a culture of cybersecurity within an organization involves instilling a collective responsibility for safeguarding digital assets. This goes beyond IT professionals, encompassing all employees at every level.

Creating awareness of cybersecurity best practices, promoting a security-conscious mindset, and encouraging a culture of reporting incidents are critical components of a comprehensive cybersecurity strategy.

Balancing Security and Innovation

In the dynamic realm of IT and digital marketing, innovation is a driving force for success. However, the pursuit of innovation often clashes with the imperative to maintain robust cybersecurity measures. Striking the right balance between security and innovation is a challenge faced by IT professionals, as they strive to enable progress without compromising the integrity of digital systems.

1. Incorporating Security by Design

Embedding security into the design and development processes from the outset is a proactive approach to mitigating cybersecurity risks. By adopting a "security by design" philosophy, IT professionals can identify and address vulnerabilities early in the development lifecycle, reducing the likelihood of security breaches later on. This approach aligns security with innovation rather than treating it as an afterthought.

2. Threat Intelligence and Proactive Defense

To stay ahead of cyber threats, IT professionals leverage threat intelligence to anticipate and prepare for potential attacks. Proactive defense involves monitoring for emerging threats, analyzing patterns, and implementing preemptive measures to mitigate risks. By adopting a proactive stance, IT professionals can minimize the impact of cyber threats and fortify digital defenses.

Conclusion

As guardians of the digital realm, IT professionals face a complex and ever-evolving landscape of cybersecurity challenges. From the escalating sophistication of cyber threats to the imperative of regulatory compliance and the delicate balance between security and innovation, the challenges are multifaceted. In this ongoing battle, continuous learning, proactive defense strategies, and a cultural commitment to cybersecurity are paramount. The future of IT and digital marketing hinges on the ability of these guardians to adapt, innovate, and fortify the defenses that protect the integrity and privacy of the digital world.

Introduction

In the rapidly evolving landscape of IT and digital marketing, navigating the intricate web of regulatory frameworks has become a paramount challenge for businesses. The increasing prevalence of data breaches, cyber threats, and privacy concerns has prompted governments worldwide to enact stringent regulations aimed at safeguarding sensitive information. This article delves into the complexities of regulatory compliance in IT, with a particular focus on industries governed by strict data protection and privacy requirements.

Understanding the Regulatory Landscape

The regulatory landscape governing IT and digital marketing is a patchwork quilt of laws and standards, each designed to address specific aspects of data protection and privacy. From the European Union's General Data Protection Regulation (GDPR) to the California Consumer Privacy Act (CCPA), businesses are confronted with a myriad of legal obligations. Navigating this complex terrain requires a comprehensive understanding of the intricacies of each regulation, as well as the ability to adapt to evolving compliance requirements.

The GDPR Challenge

The GDPR, enacted in 2018, represents a watershed moment in data protection regulation. Applicable not only to EU member states but also to any organization processing the data of EU citizens, the GDPR imposes strict requirements on the collection, processing, and storage of personal information. Achieving compliance with the GDPR involves implementing robust data protection measures, appointing a Data Protection Officer (DPO), and ensuring transparency in data processing activities. Non-compliance can result in hefty fines, making adherence to the GDPR a top priority for businesses operating in the EU and beyond.

CCPA and the U.S. Regulatory Landscape

In the United States, the CCPA introduced a new paradigm for data protection. Enacted in 2018, this regulation grants California residents greater control over their personal information held by businesses. The CCPA mandates transparent data practices, the right to opt-out of data sales, and the right to request the deletion of personal information. As other states follow suit with their own privacy laws, businesses must grapple with a complex regulatory landscape that lacks uniformity.

Data Localization and Cross-Border Challenges

One of the key challenges in regulatory compliance is the issue of data localization. Some regulations, such as Russia's data localization law, require businesses to store and process certain types of data within the country's borders. This presents a significant hurdle for multinational companies accustomed to centralized data management. Cross-border data transfers, especially in cloud-based environments, further complicate compliance efforts. Striking a balance between the need for global data flows and adherence to local regulations is a delicate task.

Balancing Innovation with Compliance

The fast-paced nature of the IT and digital marketing industries often clashes with the inherently slow-moving regulatory landscape. Innovations such as artificial intelligence, machine learning, and advanced analytics bring tremendous opportunities but also pose new challenges in terms of compliance. As businesses strive to stay ahead of the curve, they must concurrently assess the regulatory implications of adopting cutting-edge technologies. Balancing innovation with compliance requires a forward-thinking approach that anticipates potential legal and ethical pitfalls.

Cybersecurity and Regulatory Compliance

The symbiotic relationship between cybersecurity and regulatory compliance is a critical aspect of navigating the compliance tightrope. Regulatory frameworks often include specific requirements for data security, necessitating the implementation of robust cybersecurity measures. Businesses must adopt a proactive stance, regularly assessing and enhancing their cybersecurity posture to not only protect sensitive information but also to meet the stringent security standards mandated by regulations.

The Role of Privacy by Design

An emerging concept gaining prominence in the realm of regulatory compliance is "privacy by design". This principle advocates for the integration of privacy considerations into the entire lifecycle of products, systems, and processes. By embedding privacy from the outset, businesses can minimize the risk of non-compliance and demonstrate a commitment to ethical data practices. Privacy by design is not only a compliance strategy but also a proactive approach to building trust with customers and stakeholders.

The Human Factor: Training and Awareness

While technological solutions play a crucial role in achieving compliance, the human factor remains a linchpin in the overall strategy. Employees at all levels must be well-versed in data protection principles and the specific requirements of relevant regulations. Ongoing training programs and awareness campaigns are essential components of a robust compliance framework. Employees should understand their roles in safeguarding data, recognizing potential risks, and reporting incidents promptly.

The Cost of Non-Compliance

The consequences of non-compliance with regulatory frameworks can be severe, ranging from financial penalties to reputational damage. Regulatory bodies are increasingly vigilant, and the public is more attuned to issues of data privacy. A single data breach or violation of privacy regulations can lead to a loss of customer trust and confidence. The financial impact of fines, legal fees, and remediation efforts can be crippling for businesses. Thus, the cost of non-compliance extends beyond monetary penalties to encompass broader implications for the organization's viability and standing in the marketplace.

Conclusion

In the complex realm of IT and digital marketing, businesses must walk a tightrope to ensure compliance with an ever-expanding web of regulatory frameworks. The convergence of global and regional regulations, coupled with the rapid pace of technological innovation, makes this task especially challenging. Successful navigation of the compliance tightrope requires a multi-faceted approach encompassing legal expertise, technological solutions, organizational culture, and a commitment to ethical data practices. By understanding the nuances of regulatory requirements and proactively addressing potential challenges, businesses can not only meet compliance obligations but also foster trust, resilience, and sustainability in an era where data protection and privacy are paramount.

Introduction

In the fast-paced and dynamic landscape of IT and digital marketing, effective communication is paramount for success. However, one of the persistent challenges that organizations face is the communication gap between IT professionals and non-technical stakeholders. This divide often stems from the prevalent use of interdepartmental jargon, creating a barrier that hinders collaboration and understanding. In this article, we will explore the roots of this communication gap, its impact on projects, and strategies to foster effective collaboration.

Understanding the Communication Gap

1. The Language Divide

The IT department often operates in a world of acronyms, technical terms, and complex frameworks that can be intimidating for those not well-versed in the field. Digital marketing professionals, on the other hand, speak the language of campaigns, conversion rates, and customer engagement. The clash of these two distinct languages creates a communication gap that can lead to misunderstandings, delays, and even project failures.

2. Misalignment of Goals

IT teams are primarily focused on ensuring system functionality, security, and scalability. Meanwhile, digital marketing teams are driven by goals such as increasing brand visibility, driving traffic, and optimizing user experiences. The misalignment of these objectives can result in conflicting priorities and a lack of synergy, making it crucial to bridge the gap between these seemingly disparate goals.

Impact on Projects and Organizational Efficiency

1. Delayed Project Timelines

Miscommunication often leads to project delays. For instance, a marketing team might request a feature without understanding the technical complexities involved. The IT team, in turn, might implement a solution that doesn't align with the marketing strategy, resulting in iterations and delays that impact project timelines.

2. Reduced Innovation

Effective collaboration fosters innovation. When IT and marketing teams fail to communicate seamlessly, opportunities for groundbreaking solutions are missed. The synergy of technical expertise and marketing insights is essential for creating innovative products and campaigns that resonate with the target audience.

3. Increased Risk of Errors

Inadequate communication increases the risk of errors. If marketing professionals fail to convey their requirements clearly, the IT team may develop a solution that falls short of expectations. This not only affects the quality of the end product but also jeopardizes the overall success of the project.

Strategies for Bridging the Gap

1. Establishing Common Ground

To foster effective collaboration, it's essential to establish a common understanding between IT and marketing teams. This involves creating a glossary of terms that both technical and non-technical stakeholders can refer to. This simple yet effective step ensures that everyone is on the same page and reduces the likelihood of misunderstandings.

2. Cross-Training Initiatives

Organizations can invest in cross-training initiatives to enhance the understanding of each department's functions. This involves IT professionals gaining insights into digital marketing strategies and vice versa. By breaking down the silos and promoting cross-functional knowledge, teams can work together more cohesively.

3. Facilitating Open Communication Channels

Encouraging open communication channels is crucial for addressing misunderstandings promptly. Establishing regular meetings, using collaboration tools, and fostering a culture of transparency can help create an environment where team members feel comfortable expressing their thoughts and concerns.

4. Project Management Integration

Integrating project management tools that cater to both IT and marketing requirements can streamline workflows. These tools should provide a centralized platform for collaboration, allowing teams to track progress, share updates, and address issues in real-time.

5. Leadership Involvement

Leadership plays a pivotal role in bridging the communication gap. Executives and managers should actively promote a culture of collaboration, set clear expectations for communication, and provide the necessary resources for training and development.

The Road Ahead

As organizations navigate the challenges of IT and digital marketing integration, it's imperative to recognize the role of effective communication in achieving seamless collaboration. The investment in bridging the communication gap is not just about overcoming linguistic barriers; it's about creating a culture where IT and marketing professionals can leverage each other's strengths to drive innovation and success.

By addressing the root causes of interdepartmental jargon and implementing strategies to enhance communication, organizations can break down silos, reduce project delays, and foster an environment conducive to creativity and efficiency. The future of IT and digital marketing lies in the hands of organizations that prioritize collaboration and recognize the transformative power of effective communication.

Introduction

In today's fast-paced and ever-evolving business landscape, the alignment of IT initiatives with overall business goals has become a critical factor for success. The seamless integration of Information Technology (IT) with business strategy not only enhances operational efficiency but also contributes to strategic decision-making and innovation. This article explores the methods and strategies that organizations can adopt to align their IT initiatives with broader business objectives, fostering a more cohesive and mutually beneficial relationship between IT and the rest of the business.

In the digital era, where technology serves as a catalyst for business transformation, the alignment of IT and business has become a strategic imperative. The traditional perception of IT as a mere support function is evolving into a more dynamic and integrated role. Organizations that successfully align their IT initiatives with business objectives gain a competitive edge by leveraging technology to drive innovation, efficiency, and agility.

Understanding the Business Landscape

One of the foundational steps in achieving IT and business alignment is gaining a deep understanding of the business landscape. IT leaders need to be well-versed in the company's overall strategy, objectives, and challenges. This involves close collaboration between IT and business leaders to ensure that technology decisions are not made in isolation but are grounded in a comprehensive understanding of the organization's goals.

Building a Strategic IT Roadmap

A strategic IT roadmap acts as a guiding framework that aligns technology initiatives with business priorities. This involves identifying key business drivers and mapping them to specific IT initiatives. The roadmap should be flexible enough to accommodate changes in business strategy and technology trends while providing a clear direction for IT investments and projects. Regular reviews and updates ensure that IT remains in sync with evolving business needs.

Effective Communication and Collaboration

Communication is at the heart of successful IT and business alignment. IT leaders must establish effective channels for communication between IT teams and other business units. Regular meetings, collaborative platforms, and cross-functional teams can facilitate a shared understanding of goals and challenges. This open line of communication helps IT professionals stay informed about business priorities, enabling them to tailor their initiatives accordingly.

Establishing Key Performance Indicators (KPIs)

Quantifiable metrics are essential for tracking the success of IT initiatives in contributing to overall business objectives. By establishing Key Performance Indicators (KPIs) that align with strategic goals, organizations can measure the impact of IT projects on key business outcomes. This data-driven approach not only demonstrates the value of IT to the business but also provides insights for continuous improvement.

Agile Methodology and Flexibility

Agile methodology is a project management and product development approach that prioritizes flexibility, collaboration, and customer satisfaction. It involves iterative and incremental development, where teams work in short cycles, called sprints, and continuously adapt to changing requirements. Agile emphasizes customer feedback, close collaboration between cross-functional teams, and the ability to respond quickly to evolving needs throughout the development process.

In a rapidly changing business environment, agility is a key component of successful IT and business alignment. Adopting Agile methodologies allows IT teams to respond quickly to changing business requirements. The iterative nature of Agile development ensures that technology solutions remain adaptable and can evolve in tandem with shifting organizational priorities.

Investing in Employee Training and Development

A workforce that is well-versed in both IT and business practices is crucial for alignment success. Investing in training programs that bridge the gap between technical and business knowledge equips employees with the skills needed to understand and contribute to the broader business context. This, in turn, fosters a culture of collaboration and shared responsibility for achieving organizational goals.

Cultivating a Culture of Innovation

Alignment between IT and business is not just about meeting current objectives; it's also about anticipating future needs. Cultivating a culture of innovation encourages IT teams to proactively explore new technologies and propose solutions that can drive business growth. By fostering a mindset of continuous improvement and experimentation, organizations can position themselves at the forefront of industry innovation.

Risk Management and Compliance

Successful IT and business alignment must also take into account risk management and compliance considerations. IT initiatives should be designed with a keen awareness of potential risks and compliance requirements. By incorporating risk assessments into the decision-making process, organizations can avoid pitfalls that could hinder the achievement of business objectives.

Measuring Return on Investment (ROI)

To demonstrate the tangible benefits of IT initiatives, organizations must measure and communicate the return on investment (ROI). This involves not only financial metrics but also qualitative measures such as improved customer satisfaction, increased employee productivity, and enhanced competitive positioning. A comprehensive ROI analysis provides stakeholders with a clear picture of how IT investments contribute to overall business success.

Conclusion

In the face of evolving technologies and dynamic market conditions, IT and business alignment is not a one-time achievement but an ongoing process. Organizations that prioritize this alignment gain a strategic advantage by leveraging technology to drive innovation, improve efficiency, and achieve business goals. By fostering a culture of collaboration, investing in employee development, and embracing agile methodologies, businesses can position themselves to thrive in the digital age. Understanding and implementing these strategies will be crucial for organizations seeking to navigate the complexities of the modern business landscape.

Introduction

In the dynamic realms of IT and digital marketing, where innovation is the driving force, projects often encounter the formidable challenge of scope creep. Scope creep refers to the uncontrolled expansion of project requirements, often resulting in unforeseen obstacles that can jeopardize timelines, inflate costs, and strain resource allocation. This article delves into the complexities of scope changes and their profound impact on project management within the IT and digital marketing domains.

Understanding Scope Creep

Scope creep is a common menace in project management, characterized by the gradual addition of new features, functionalities, or tasks that were not initially included in the project plan. This phenomenon arises from evolving stakeholder expectations, unclear project objectives, or inadequate communication channels. As the project progresses, stakeholders may realize new possibilities or encounter emerging challenges, leading to a desire for modifications and additions to the original scope.

The Impact on Project Timelines

One of the most immediate and palpable consequences of scope creep is its adverse effect on project timelines. The inclusion of new elements without a corresponding extension of deadlines can lead to rushed implementations, compromised quality, and increased risk of errors. Delays in project delivery not only frustrate stakeholders but also hinder the project's overall success. Managing scope changes effectively is crucial to mitigating the risks associated with timeline disruptions.

The Butterfly Effect of Scope Creep

The butterfly effect is a concept in chaos theory that suggests a small change or action in one part of a system can have far-reaching and unpredictable consequences in other parts of the system. The term is often used metaphorically to illustrate how a seemingly minor event or decision can lead to significant and unexpected outcomes over time. The butterfly effect highlights the sensitivity and interdependence of complex systems.

Consider a digital marketing campaign aimed at launching a new product. Initially scoped for a three-month timeline, the project encounters scope creep when stakeholders decide to incorporate an additional social media platform for promotion. Without extending the project deadline, the team is forced to divide their attention, leading to suboptimal results on both platforms. The butterfly effect of scope creep becomes evident as delays cascade through subsequent project phases, affecting overall campaign performance.

The Escalation of Costs

Scope changes invariably contribute to an escalation of project costs. Additional features or functionalities may require extra resources, whether in the form of manpower, technology, or tools. Failure to anticipate these added expenses can strain the project budget, leading to financial challenges for both the project team and the organization as a whole. Effective cost management demands a proactive approach to identifying and accommodating changes in scope to prevent budget overruns.

Navigating Budgetary Challenges

To illustrate the impact of scope changes on project costs, let's examine an IT project tasked with developing a custom software solution. Midway through the project, stakeholders request the inclusion of a new feature to enhance user experience. Without a thorough assessment of the associated costs, the project team encounters unexpected expenses for additional development hours and testing resources. The failure to factor in these costs from the outset results in budgetary challenges and potential compromises in other project areas.

Resource Allocation Strain

Scope creep not only affects timelines and costs but also places a strain on resource allocation. The unplanned inclusion of new tasks can lead to overburdened teams, divided attention, and compromised efficiency. Project managers must navigate the delicate balance of meeting stakeholder expectations while ensuring that the available resources are optimally utilized. Failure to address resource allocation challenges can result in burnout, decreased morale, and a decline in the overall quality of project deliverables.

Strategies for Managing Scope Creep

Effectively managing scope creep requires a combination of proactive planning, clear communication, and robust change control processes. The following strategies can help mitigate the impact of scope changes on IT and digital marketing projects.

1. Thorough Requirements Analysis

Before the project begins, conduct a comprehensive analysis of requirements with stakeholders. Clarify expectations, identify potential changes, and establish a clear scope definition. This proactive approach lays the foundation for a more predictable project trajectory.

2. Clear Communication Channels

Establish and maintain open communication channels with stakeholders throughout the project lifecycle. Encourage stakeholders to express their expectations and concerns early on, fostering a collaborative environment where changes can be discussed and evaluated promptly.

3. Documented Change Control Processes

Implement a robust change control process that requires stakeholders to formally document and justify any proposed changes to the project scope. This documentation should include an assessment of the impact on timelines, costs, and resources.

4. Regular Progress Reviews

Conduct regular progress reviews with stakeholders to assess the project's alignment with initial goals. These reviews provide opportunities to identify potential scope changes early and evaluate their feasibility within the project's constraints.

5. Flexibility within Constraints

Acknowledge that some degree of change is inevitable in dynamic environments. However, maintain a balance by evaluating the feasibility of scope changes within the constraints of timelines, costs, and resource availability.

Conclusion

In the ever-evolving landscape of IT and digital marketing, scope creep poses a significant challenge to project success. The impact on timelines, costs, and resource allocation can be profound, necessitating a proactive and strategic approach to scope management. By embracing clear communication, robust change control processes, and a commitment to thorough planning, project managers can navigate the complexities of scope creep and ensure the successful delivery of IT and digital marketing initiatives. As organizations continue to innovate and adapt to market dynamics, mastering the art of scope management becomes a critical skill in overcoming the persistent pains associated with project execution in these dynamic domains.

Introduction

In the ever-evolving landscape of IT and digital marketing, one of the most formidable challenges faced by professionals is the relentless ticking of project clocks. Tight timelines have become a hallmark of this industry, where the pace of innovation and the demand for quick turnarounds often set the tone for success or failure. This article delves into the nuances of managing tight deadlines, exploring the impact on project management and the well-being of IT professionals.

The Need for Speed

In the fast-paced world of IT and digital marketing, the need for speed is not just a cliché but a fundamental reality. Businesses are under constant pressure to stay ahead of the curve, and technology evolves at a breakneck pace. As a result, projects are often initiated with timelines that seem ambitious at best. The urgency to launch new products, implement cutting-edge technologies, or respond to market dynamics places an immense burden on project teams to deliver results swiftly.

Project Management Under the Gun

Managing projects within tight timelines requires a delicate balance of planning, execution, and adaptability. Project managers find themselves in the challenging position of orchestrating complex workflows while ensuring that every team member is aligned with the project's goals and deadlines. The traditional project management triangle -

scope, time, and cost - becomes a high-stakes game where any adjustment in one parameter affects the others.

Project managers must navigate through the constraints imposed by tight timelines, often making tough decisions about prioritizing tasks, allocating resources, and adjusting project scopes. The pressure to meet deadlines can lead to a heightened risk of burnout among project managers, who find themselves juggling multiple responsibilities while attempting to keep the project on course.

The Domino Effect on Team Dynamics

The ripple effect of tight timelines extends beyond project managers to impact the entire team. Collaboration and effective communication become even more critical in this environment, as delays or missteps in one area can have cascading effects on the entire project. Team members may find themselves stretched thin, working long hours to meet deadlines and sacrificing work-life balance in the process.

The dynamics of teamwork can be strained under the weight of tight timelines. The stress of looming deadlines may lead to increased tension among team members, impacting morale and creativity. In a race against the clock, the quality of collaboration can suffer, potentially compromising the overall success of the project.

Quality vs. Speed Dilemma

One of the most significant challenges posed by tight timelines is the inherent trade-off between speed and quality. The pressure to deliver results quickly can tempt teams to cut corners, compromise on testing procedures, or overlook critical details. While meeting deadlines is imperative, sacrificing quality can have long-term consequences, leading to post-implementation issues, customer dissatisfaction, and even reputational damage.

IT professionals must grapple with the dilemma of finding the right balance between speed and quality. Striking this balance requires a thoughtful approach to project planning, resource allocation, and risk management. The challenge lies in resisting the allure of shortcuts that may provide short-term gains but jeopardize the project's overall success.

Innovation Amidst Constraints

Tight timelines can be both a driver and a hindrance to innovation. On one hand, the urgency to meet deadlines can spur creative problem-solving and push teams to think outside the box. On the other hand, the relentless focus on timelines may stifle the ideation phase, limiting the exploration of unconventional and groundbreaking ideas.

Innovation thrives in an environment that encourages experimentation and embraces the unknown. IT professionals navigating tight timelines must find ways to foster creativity within the constraints imposed by project clocks. Balancing the need for innovation with the demands of tight deadlines requires a strategic approach that incorporates flexibility and adaptability into the project lifecycle.

The Toll on Professional Well-Being

The relentless race against project clocks takes a toll on the well-being of IT professionals. Long hours, high stress levels, and the constant pressure to deliver results can lead to burnout - a pervasive issue in the industry. Burnout not only affects individual professionals but also poses a risk to the overall health and productivity of the team.

The IT sector, known for its dynamic and demanding nature, must prioritize the well-being of its workforce. Employers need to implement strategies that promote a healthy work-life balance, provide adequate support for mental health, and recognize the signs of burnout before it reaches a critical stage. Investing in the well-being of IT professionals is not just a matter of corporate responsibility but also a strategic imperative for sustaining long-term success.

Strategies for Success in the Race Against Time

While tight timelines present formidable challenges, they are not insurmountable. Successful navigation of the race against project clocks requires a combination of strategic planning, effective communication, and a commitment to the well-being of the project team. Here are some key strategies for success.

Prioritize and Sequence Tasks: Clearly identify project priorities and sequence tasks based on their criticality. This ensures that essential components are addressed first, reducing the risk of delays impacting the overall project timeline.

Embrace Agile Methodologies: Agile methodologies, with their iterative and flexible approach, are well-suited for projects with tight timelines. Embracing agility allows teams to adapt to changing requirements and deliver incremental value throughout the project lifecycle.

Implement Effective Communication Channels: Open and transparent communication is crucial when working under tight timelines. Establishing effective communication channels ensures that team members are well-informed, potential issues are identified early, and adjustments can be made promptly.

Invest in Automation and Tools: Leveraging automation and project management tools can streamline workflows and enhance efficiency. Automation reduces manual effort, minimizes the risk of errors, and accelerates processes, contributing to meeting tight deadlines.

Cultivate a Supportive Work Culture: Fostering a work culture that prioritizes collaboration, recognizes achievements, and supports the well-being of team members is essential. A positive work environment enhances motivation and resilience, even in the face of tight timelines.

Conclusion

In the challenging landscape of IT and digital marketing, tight timelines have become a defining feature of project management. The race against project clocks demands a delicate balance between speed, quality, and the well-being of IT professionals. Successfully navigating this race requires strategic planning, effective communication, and a commitment to fostering a supportive work culture.

As the industry continues to evolve, IT professionals and project managers must adapt to the demands of tight timelines while ensuring that innovation, quality, and individual well-being are not sacrificed in the process. The race against project clocks is a marathon, not a sprint, and success lies in finding the right pace that balances urgency with sustainability.

Introduction

In the dynamic realm of digital marketing, where algorithms are the gatekeepers to visibility and success, marketers find themselves on an ever-shifting landscape. The intricate dance between marketers and algorithms has become a central theme in the narrative of online promotion. In this article, we embark on a journey through the algorithmic adventures of digital marketing, exploring the profound impact of frequent algorithm updates on strategies and tactics employed by marketers to stay ahead in the game.

Understanding the Algorithmic Landscape

Digital marketing platforms, from search engines to social media giants, operate on complex algorithms that determine the content users see. These algorithms are designed to deliver personalized and relevant content, creating a user experience that keeps individuals engaged. However, this intricate dance has profound implications for marketers, as the algorithms wield significant influence over the visibility of their content.

The Algorithmic Evolution

Algorithms are not static; they evolve continuously. The major players in the digital landscape, such as Google and Facebook, regularly update their algorithms to enhance user experience, weed out spam, and adapt to changing trends. These updates, while serving the broader goal of improving user satisfaction, often send shockwaves through the digital marketing community.

Impact of Algorithm Updates on Search Engine Optimization (SEO)

1. The Google Dance

The term "Google Dance" refers to the period when Google's search engine rankings fluctuate dramatically during an update, causing significant changes in website positions within the search results.

For SEO professionals, the term "Google Dance" is not a whimsical affair but a reflection of the volatility induced by algorithm updates. Google's search algorithm, in particular, undergoes frequent updates, affecting the ranking of websites in search results. Marketers engaged in SEO practices must constantly adjust their strategies to align with these algorithmic shifts.

2. Quality Over Quantity

Historically, SEO was often about gaming the system - loading content with keywords to climb the search rankings. However, algorithm updates in recent years have emphasized quality over quantity. Content relevance, user experience, and authenticity are now paramount. Marketers must focus on producing content that genuinely addresses user needs, navigating the delicate balance between optimization for algorithms and creating valuable content for humans.

Social Media Algorithms

1. The Visibility Challenge

Social media platforms, with their algorithmic feeds, pose a unique challenge for marketers. Algorithm updates on platforms like Facebook and Instagram can dramatically alter the visibility of content. Marketers, who once relied on organic reach, now find their posts reaching a smaller audience unless they align with the algorithms' preferences.

2. Engaging Content Wins

To navigate the evolving landscape of social media algorithms, marketers must prioritize creating engaging and shareable content. Algorithms favor content that sparks conversations and interactions, and marketers need to understand the nuances of each platform's algorithm to tailor their content accordingly. The days of simply broadcasting messages to a passive audience are long gone; today, it's about building communities and fostering engagement.

The E-Commerce Dilemma

1. Personalization Imperative

E-commerce platforms rely heavily on algorithms to provide users with personalized product recommendations. While this enhances the user experience, it adds a layer of complexity for marketers. Understanding the algorithms governing product suggestions becomes crucial for optimizing product visibility and driving sales.

2. Algorithmic Advertising

In the world of e-commerce, paid advertising is a key strategy. Algorithms play a pivotal role in determining the success of these campaigns. Marketers must constantly analyze data, tweak ad targeting parameters, and adapt their approaches to align with algorithmic preferences, ensuring their ads are served to the right audience at the right time.

Navigating the Algorithmic Seas

1. Continuous Adaptation

In the face of ever-changing algorithms, the ability to adapt is a marketer's greatest asset. Staying informed about algorithm updates, understanding their implications, and adjusting strategies accordingly is essential. This requires a commitment to continuous learning and a nimble approach to campaign management.

2. Data-Driven Decision Making

Algorithms are driven by data, and marketers must harness the power of data analytics to inform their strategies. Regularly analyzing performance metrics, user behavior, and engagement data can provide valuable insights into how algorithms are responding to content. This data-driven approach enables marketers to make informed decisions and refine their tactics.

3. Diversification of Platforms

Relying solely on one digital marketing platform is a risky proposition. Algorithm updates on a single platform can have a profound impact on a business's visibility. Diversifying across multiple platforms helps spread the risk and provides a more resilient marketing strategy. Each platform has its own algorithmic nuances, and diversification ensures that marketers can adapt to changes on any given platform.

The Future of Algorithmic Adventures

1. AI and Machine Learning

As technology advances, the role of artificial intelligence (AI) and machine learning in shaping algorithms is becoming more pronounced. Predictive algorithms that anticipate user behavior and preferences are on the horizon. Marketers need to prepare for a future where algorithms become even more sophisticated, requiring a deeper understanding of AI-driven decision-making processes.

2. Ethical Considerations

The increasing influence of algorithms in shaping online experiences raises ethical questions. The responsibility of marketers extends beyond optimizing for algorithms; it involves a commitment to ethical practices. As algorithms become more powerful, marketers must be mindful of the potential impact on user privacy, transparency, and the unintended consequences of algorithmic decision-making.

Conclusion

In the vast ocean of digital marketing, algorithms are the currents that shape the landscape. Navigating the algorithmic adventures requires marketers to be agile, data-driven, and ethically conscious. The impact of frequent algorithm updates is not just a challenge; it's an opportunity for marketers to innovate, learn, and refine their strategies. As the digital marketing landscape continues to evolve, those who master the art of sailing through the algorithmic waves will find themselves at the forefront of success in the ever-expanding realm of online promotion.

Chapter 10. Data Privacy Dilemmas in the Digital Age

Introduction

In the ever-evolving landscape of IT and digital marketing, data privacy has emerged as a critical concern, posing significant challenges for businesses aiming to thrive in the digital age. As technology advances and consumer data becomes more accessible, the ethical and legal dimensions of data privacy have taken center stage. This article explores the complex web of data privacy dilemmas in the digital age, shedding light on the challenges that digital marketers encounter in ensuring compliance and fostering consumer trust.

The digital age has witnessed an unprecedented surge in the collection, processing, and utilization of personal data. From targeted advertising to personalized user experiences, businesses leverage consumer data to gain a competitive edge. However, this digital transformation comes at a cost - the erosion of privacy. As consumers become increasingly aware of the value of their data, the demand for robust data privacy measures has skyrocketed.

The Regulatory Landscape

One of the foremost challenges for digital marketers is the intricate web of data privacy regulations. Laws such as the General Data Protection Regulation (GDPR) in Europe and the California Consumer Privacy Act (CCPA) in the United States have ushered in a new era of compliance. Navigating these regulations requires a deep understanding of the legal landscape, as non-compliance can result in severe penalties.

The challenge lies not only in adhering to these regulations but also in staying abreast of the evolving legal framework.

Consent Conundrum

Obtaining user consent for data collection is a delicate balancing act. On one hand, marketers strive to provide personalized experiences tailored to individual preferences. On the other, obtaining explicit consent without overwhelming users with lengthy, jargon-filled consent forms is a constant challenge. Digital marketers must find innovative ways to communicate the value of data collection to users and make the consent process transparent and user-friendly.

Data Security Imperatives

The digital era has brought about an alarming increase in cyber threats and data breaches. For digital marketers, safeguarding consumer data is not just a legal requirement but a crucial aspect of maintaining trust. The challenge lies in implementing robust cybersecurity measures to protect against evolving threats. From encryption protocols to secure data storage, marketers must prioritize data security to mitigate the risk of breaches and protect consumer trust.

Third-Party Perils

Digital marketers often rely on third-party vendors for various services, from analytics to ad targeting. However, this reliance introduces another layer of complexity in ensuring data privacy. Marketers must scrutinize the data practices of their vendors, ensuring they comply with privacy regulations and adhere to ethical standards. The challenge lies in maintaining control over data when it traverses through various third-party systems, preventing unauthorized access and ensuring accountability throughout the data lifecycle.

Ethical Dilemmas

In the pursuit of business goals, digital marketers face ethical dilemmas regarding the use of consumer data. The challenge is to strike a balance between leveraging data for targeted marketing and respecting user privacy. Building and maintaining consumer trust require marketers to adopt transparent and ethical practices. Any misstep in this regard can lead to reputational damage, impacting brand loyalty and customer retention.

Data Minimization and Retention

While data is a valuable asset, the principle of data minimization poses a challenge for digital marketers. Collecting only the necessary data for a specific purpose is a fundamental tenet of privacy compliance. However, marketers often grapple with the temptation to amass extensive datasets for future use. Striking a balance between data minimization and retaining enough information for effective marketing strategies is a constant challenge, requiring a nuanced approach.

Educating Internal Stakeholders

Ensuring data privacy is not solely the responsibility of the legal or IT department; it permeates every facet of an organization. Educating internal stakeholders, from marketing teams to top management, is a crucial challenge. Marketers need to understand the implications of their actions on data privacy, and management must prioritize and invest in comprehensive training programs. Bridging the knowledge gap within the organization is imperative for building a culture that values and protects consumer data.

Transparency as a Trust-Building Tool

Transparency is the cornerstone of building and maintaining consumer trust in the digital age. Marketers face the challenge of communicating their data practices clearly and openly to consumers. This involves not only being transparent about how data is collected and used but also about the measures taken to ensure its security. Marketers who can successfully navigate this challenge stand to gain a competitive advantage by fostering trust and loyalty among their customer base.

Conclusion

In the dynamic realm of IT and digital marketing, data privacy dilemmas are here to stay. Navigating this complex landscape requires a holistic approach that combines legal compliance, ethical considerations, and a commitment to transparency. Digital marketers must view data privacy not merely as a regulatory hurdle but as an opportunity to build lasting relationships with consumers based on trust and respect.

As the digital age continues to unfold, the challenges of data privacy will evolve, demanding continuous adaptation and innovation from digital marketers. By embracing these challenges head-on, organizations can not only comply with regulations but also differentiate themselves by placing consumer privacy at the forefront of their digital strategies. In doing so, they will not only survive but thrive in the ever-changing landscape of IT and digital marketing.

Introduction

In the ever-evolving realm of IT and digital marketing, one challenge that has become increasingly prevalent is the phenomenon of content overload. As technology continues to advance and the digital space becomes more crowded, businesses and marketers find themselves grappling with the difficulty of standing out amidst the incessant noise. In this article, we will explore the intricacies of content overload, its implications, and most importantly, strategies for creating and promoting high-quality, engaging content that can cut through the clutter.

Understanding the Content Overload Dilemma

The digital era has ushered in an unprecedented flood of information. From social media updates to blog posts, videos, podcasts, and more, consumers are bombarded with content from all directions. The sheer volume of information available has led to a saturation point, making it challenging for businesses to capture the attention of their target audience. As a result, many valuable pieces of content get lost in the noise, diminishing their impact and rendering them ineffective.

The Impact on IT and Digital Marketing

Content overload poses a significant challenge for professionals in the realms of IT and digital marketing. As businesses strive to establish their online presence, the struggle to create content that resonates with their audience intensifies. This saturation not only affects the reach of the content but also contributes to audience fatigue. Consumers are becoming more discerning, filtering out content that doesn't immediately capture their interest, and this makes it even more difficult for businesses to connect with their target demographic.

Strategies for Crafting High-Quality Content

1. Audience-Centric Approach

To rise above the noise, it is crucial to adopt an audience-centric approach to content creation. Understanding the needs, preferences, and pain points of the target audience is the first step towards developing content that truly resonates. Conducting thorough research, surveys, and data analysis can provide valuable insights into what your audience is looking for and how they consume information.

2. Quality Over Quantity

In the era of content overload, the emphasis should shift from churning out a high volume of content to creating high-quality, meaningful pieces. Instead of focusing on the frequency of content production, businesses should invest time and resources in crafting well-researched, informative, and engaging content that adds genuine value to the audience. This approach not only sets your content apart but also establishes credibility and authority in your niche.

3. Diversification of Content Formats

Variety is the spice of life, and the same holds true for content. Diversifying content formats can be an effective strategy to cater to different audience preferences. Incorporating videos, infographics, podcasts, and interactive content can provide a refreshing change for your audience and increase the chances of your content standing out amidst the sea of text-based information.

4. Storytelling and Authenticity

In a digital landscape inundated with information, stories have the power to captivate and resonate on a deeper level. Incorporating storytelling into your content humanizes your brand and makes it more relatable. Authenticity is equally crucial; consumers can discern when content is forced or insincere. Being genuine in your communication fosters trust and loyalty among your audience.

5. Search Engine Optimization (SEO) Practices

Amidst the content overload, ensuring your content is discoverable is paramount. Implementing effective SEO practices helps your content rank higher in search engine results, increasing its visibility. Keyword research, optimizing meta tags, and creating compelling meta descriptions are essential elements to enhance the searchability of your content.

Promoting Your Content in a Saturated Market

Crafting high-quality content is only half the battle; effective promotion is the other key component in the quest to rise above the noise.

1. Social Media Engagement

Leveraging the power of social media is crucial for content promotion. Identifying the platforms where your target audience is most active and tailoring your content accordingly can significantly enhance its reach. Engaging with your audience through comments, shares, and discussions can also amplify the visibility of your content.

2. Influencer Collaborations

Partnering with influencers in your industry can provide a powerful boost to your content. Influencers have established credibility and a dedicated following, making them influential voices that can amplify your message. Collaborative efforts, such as guest blog posts or joint webinars, can expose your content to a broader audience.

3. Email Marketing Campaigns

Email remains a potent tool for content promotion. Building and nurturing an email subscriber list enables direct communication with your audience. Crafting compelling email campaigns with personalized content recommendations can drive engagement and increase the likelihood of your content being shared.

4. Paid Advertising Strategies

In a saturated digital landscape, strategic investment in paid advertising can be a game-changer. Platforms like Google Ads and social media advertising allow you to target specific demographics, ensuring your content reaches the right audience. Allocating budget for sponsored content or pay-per-click campaigns can boost visibility and drive traffic to your valuable content.

Measuring Success and Iterating Strategies

The digital landscape is dynamic, and what works today may not be as effective tomorrow. Therefore, measuring the success of your content and iterating your strategies based on the data is crucial for sustained relevance and impact.

1. Analytics and Key Performance Indicators (KPIs)

Utilizing analytics tools to track the performance of your content is imperative. Monitoring metrics such as website traffic, engagement rates, conversion rates, and social media analytics provides valuable insights into the effectiveness of your content strategy. Establishing clear KPIs allows you to gauge success and make data-driven decisions.

2. Feedback Loops and Adaptability

Creating feedback loops with your audience through surveys, comments, and direct feedback channels fosters a culture of continuous improvement. Being adaptable and responsive to evolving trends and audience preferences ensures that your content remains relevant and resonant.

Conclusion

In the face of content overload, the challenges in IT and digital marketing are undeniably complex. However, by adopting a strategic and audience-centric approach, businesses can navigate the digital terrain successfully. Crafting high-quality content and promoting it effectively require a holistic understanding of the target audience, industry trends, and the ever-changing dynamics of the digital landscape. Embracing innovation, staying authentic, and remaining adaptable are the cornerstones of rising above the noise and establishing a meaningful and lasting connection with your audience in the digital age.

Introduction

In the fast-paced world of IT and digital marketing, the demand for real-time engagement has become more pronounced than ever before. Consumers, accustomed to instant gratification, expect swift and seamless interactions across various digital channels. This article delves into the challenges faced by businesses in meeting these heightened consumer expectations and explores the imperative for speed in real-time engagement.

The Changing Landscape of Consumer Expectations

The advent of technology and the proliferation of digital platforms have fundamentally altered the way consumers perceive and interact with brands. Today's consumers are not only well-informed but also inherently impatient. Whether browsing an e-commerce site, seeking customer support, or interacting on social media, they demand immediate responses and personalized experiences.

1. Rising Expectations in the Digital Age

Consumers now expect businesses to be available 24/7, responding to queries, addressing concerns, and delivering personalized content in real-time. This shift in expectations is fueled by the seamless experiences offered by tech giants and agile startups, setting a new benchmark for customer engagement across industries.

2. The Multichannel Challenge

Real-time engagement is not limited to a single channel. Businesses must contend with consumers who seamlessly transition between websites, social media, mobile apps, and more. Maintaining consistency and responsiveness across these diverse channels poses a significant challenge.

3. Balancing Personalization and Privacy

As businesses strive to provide real-time, personalized experiences, they must navigate the delicate balance between customization and privacy. Consumers appreciate personalized content but are increasingly concerned about the security and privacy of their data. Meeting this dual challenge is essential to building and maintaining trust.

Challenges in Real-Time Engagement

1. Technological Hurdles

Implementing real-time engagement strategies requires robust technological infrastructure. Legacy systems and outdated software may hinder the ability to process and analyze data in real-time. Businesses face the challenge of integrating modern technologies seamlessly into their existing IT ecosystems.

2. Data Overload and Analysis Paralysis

The abundance of data generated in real-time can overwhelm businesses. Extracting meaningful insights from this deluge of information is a significant challenge. Additionally, the pressure to make split-second decisions based on real-time data introduces the risk of analysis paralysis (state of overthinking or overanalyzing a situation to the extent that a decision or action is never taken, leading to a lack of progress or decision-making).

3. Human Resources and Training

Ensuring that customer support teams and digital marketers are equipped to handle real-time interactions is crucial. Proper training, hiring, and retaining skilled professionals are challenges that businesses must address to maintain the quality of engagement across digital channels.

The Need for Speed in Real-Time Engagement

1. Competitive Edge

In today's hyper-competitive landscape, real-time engagement can be a key differentiator. Businesses that can respond swiftly to customer needs gain a competitive edge. The ability to provide immediate solutions and personalized experiences contributes to customer loyalty and brand advocacy.

2. Enhancing Customer Experience

Speed in real-time engagement directly correlates with the quality of customer experience. Businesses that prioritize quick and relevant responses create a positive impression, fostering customer satisfaction and loyalty. Conversely, delays or generic responses can lead to frustration and erode brand trust.

3. Adapting to Market Trends

The digital landscape is dynamic, with trends and consumer preferences evolving rapidly. Real-time engagement allows businesses to adapt quickly to market shifts, ensuring that their strategies remain relevant and effective. Staying ahead of the curve is essential for sustained success.

Strategies for Effective Real-Time Engagement

1. Leveraging AI and Automation

Artificial Intelligence (AI) and automation play a pivotal role in achieving real-time engagement. Chatbots, virtual assistants, and automated response systems enable businesses to handle a high volume of interactions simultaneously, providing instant solutions and freeing up human resources for more complex tasks.

2. Investing in Advanced Analytics

To overcome the challenges of data overload, businesses must invest in advanced analytics tools. These tools not only facilitate real-time data processing but also empower organizations to derive actionable insights, enabling informed decision-making in the blink of an eye.

3. Seamless Integration of Technologies

A holistic approach to technology integration is essential. Businesses must ensure that their CRM (Customer Relationship Management) systems, marketing platforms, and communication tools seamlessly work together to deliver a unified real-time experience. Siloed systems can impede the flow of information and hinder responsiveness.

Siloed systems refer to isolated or compartmentalized information systems within an organization that operate independently, often lacking effective communication and data sharing between them. This lack of integration can hinder collaboration, efficiency, and a unified view of information across different departments or functions within the organization.

Conclusion

The need for speed in real-time engagement has never been more critical for businesses navigating the challenges of IT and digital marketing. Consumers, with their heightened expectations, demand instant, personalized interactions across diverse digital channels. Overcoming technological hurdles, adapting to market trends, and leveraging advanced strategies are imperative for businesses aiming to thrive in this dynamic landscape. By addressing these challenges head-on and prioritizing speed in engagement, organizations can not only meet but exceed consumer expectations, building lasting relationships in the digital age.

Introduction

In the fast-evolving landscape of Information Technology (IT) and Digital Marketing, the sheer volume of data generated by digital campaigns can be overwhelming. This deluge of information, often referred to as big data, poses both a challenge and an opportunity for businesses. Deciphering this digital data and accurately measuring Return on Investment (ROI) has become a crucial aspect of ensuring the success and sustainability of digital marketing efforts.

Understanding the Digital Deluge

The first challenge in decoding digital data lies in understanding the sheer volume and diversity of information generated. From website traffic and social media interactions to email click-through rates, every digital touchpoint contributes to a vast reservoir of data. The complexity intensifies as this data comes in different formats, from structured databases to unstructured social media posts and comments. To decode this digital deluge, organizations need sophisticated tools and analytical frameworks that can process and make sense of diverse datasets.

The Role of Analytics in Decoding Digital Data

Analytics is the linchpin in the process of decoding digital data. Businesses leverage various analytical tools and techniques to transform raw data into actionable insights. Descriptive analytics provides a retrospective view, offering an overview of what has happened in the past. Diagnostic analytics delves deeper, seeking to understand why certain events occurred. Predictive analytics uses historical data to forecast future trends, while prescriptive analytics recommends actions to optimize outcomes.

In the context of digital marketing, these analytics techniques are indispensable for measuring ROI. By dissecting data from different channels, businesses can identify which aspects of their digital campaigns are driving results and which require optimization. Analytics also plays a pivotal role in attributing conversions to specific touchpoints, shedding light on the customer journey and the effectiveness of each marketing channel.

Attribution Modeling

Attribution modeling is a critical component of the ROI analysis puzzle. It involves assigning value to different touchpoints in the customer journey to understand their impact on conversions. The customer journey in the digital realm is often complex, with multiple touchpoints influencing the final decision. Attribution modeling helps in assigning credit to each touchpoint, enabling marketers to optimize their strategies based on the most impactful channels.

Common attribution models include first-touch attribution, last-touch attribution, and multi-touch attribution. First-touch attribution gives credit to the initial interaction that led to a conversion, while last-touch attribution attributes the conversion to the final touchpoint. Multi-touch attribution, on the other hand, acknowledges the contribution of multiple touchpoints in the conversion journey.

However, attributing conversions accurately is easier said than done. The rise of cross-channel marketing and the proliferation of devices have made it challenging to track a user's entire journey. The fragmented nature of digital interactions requires a nuanced approach to attribution modeling, recognizing that the customer journey is often a dynamic and non-linear process.

Challenges in Attribution Modeling

One of the primary challenges in attribution modeling is the lack of a one-size-fits-all solution. Different businesses, industries, and even individual campaigns may require unique attribution models based on their specific goals and customer behaviors. Additionally, the absence of a universal identifier for users across devices and platforms complicates the tracking process.

The rise of ad blockers and privacy regulations further complicates attribution modeling. With users actively blocking ads and demanding greater control over their data, marketers face hurdles in tracking and attributing conversions. This necessitates a reevaluation of traditional attribution models and a shift towards more privacy-conscious and user-centric approaches.

Data Quality and Integration

Decoding digital data and measuring ROI also hinge on the quality and integration of data. Inaccurate or incomplete data can lead to flawed insights and misinformed decision-making. Integration challenges arise when dealing with data from disparate sources, such as social media platforms, CRM systems, and website analytics tools.

Ensuring data quality involves regular audits, validation checks, and the implementation of data hygiene practices. Organizations must also invest in technologies that facilitate seamless data integration. The integration of data from various sources provides a holistic view of customer interactions, enabling a more accurate assessment of ROI.

The Role of Artificial Intelligence in ROI Analysis

Artificial Intelligence (AI) is emerging as a game-changer in decoding digital data and enhancing ROI analysis. Machine learning algorithms can analyze vast datasets at speed, identifying patterns and trends that may elude traditional analytical methods. AI-powered tools also facilitate predictive modeling, helping businesses anticipate customer behavior and optimize marketing strategies accordingly.

In the realm of ROI analysis, AI plays a crucial role in predictive attribution modeling. By leveraging historical data and continuously learning from new interactions, AI algorithms can provide more accurate predictions of how different touchpoints contribute to conversions. This empowers marketers to allocate budgets more effectively, focusing on the channels that are likely to yield the highest ROI.

The Future of Decoding Digital Data

As technology continues to evolve, the challenges and opportunities in decoding digital data will only intensify. The integration of emerging technologies, such as blockchain and edge computing, holds the promise of addressing some of the existing challenges in data quality, security, and privacy.

The future of ROI analysis in digital marketing will likely see a shift towards more sophisticated and dynamic attribution models. AI and machine learning will play an increasingly central role, not only in predictive modeling but also in automating routine tasks, allowing marketers to focus on strategic decision-making.

Conclusion

Decoding digital data and measuring ROI in the realm of IT and digital marketing is a multifaceted challenge that requires a strategic approach. Analytics, attribution modeling, data quality, and the integration of emerging technologies are all integral components of a successful ROI analysis framework. As businesses continue to invest heavily in digital marketing, mastering the art of decoding digital data will be paramount to staying competitive and ensuring a positive return on investment. The journey may be complex, but the insights gleaned from decoding digital data pave the way for informed decision-making and sustainable business growth in the digital era.

Chapter 14. Globalization Hurdles
Tailoring Marketing for Diverse Audiences

Introduction

In an era dominated by technological advancements and interconnectedness, the world has become a global village. As a result, businesses are expanding their reach across borders, necessitating a nuanced understanding of diverse cultural contexts and markets. The field of digital marketing, integral to modern business strategies, faces unique challenges in the realm of globalization. This article delves into the hurdles associated with adapting digital marketing strategies for diverse audiences, exploring the intricacies of cultural sensitivity, linguistic nuances, and market variations.

Understanding Cultural Sensitivity in Digital Marketing

One of the foremost challenges in global digital marketing lies in navigating the intricate web of diverse cultures. What resonates with one audience may be perceived differently by another, demanding a deep understanding of cultural sensitivities. For instance, colors, symbols, and even certain words can carry varying meanings across cultures. Successful digital marketing requires a level of cultural intelligence to ensure messages are not only understood but also well-received.

Cultural nuances extend beyond aesthetics to encompass communication styles. High-context cultures, where much of the communication is implicit, contrast with low-context cultures, where explicit communication is favored. Striking the right balance is essential in crafting content that transcends cultural barriers, resonating with audiences from different cultural backgrounds.

Language as a Barrier

In the realm of digital marketing, language is both a powerful tool and a potential stumbling block. A well-crafted message can captivate an audience, but linguistic nuances can lead to misunderstandings or, worse, unintended offense. Translating content is not a straightforward task; it requires more than just converting words from one language to another. Idioms, cultural references, and colloquialisms must be considered to ensure the message retains its intended impact.

Moreover, linguistic challenges go beyond translation. The choice of language itself can be a strategic decision. While English is widely spoken globally, local languages often hold greater sway in connecting with audiences on a personal level. Companies must decide whether to adopt a one-size-fits-all approach with a global language or invest in multilingual campaigns tailored to specific regions.

Navigating Regulatory Divergence

Globalization brings not only diverse cultures and languages but also a myriad of regulatory frameworks. Digital marketing campaigns must adhere to local laws and regulations governing data protection, advertising standards, and consumer rights. The General Data Protection Regulation (GDPR) in Europe, for example, imposes strict guidelines on the collection and processing of personal data. Failure to comply can result in severe penalties.

Moreover, cultural and societal norms influence regulatory perspectives. What may be deemed acceptable advertising content in one region could be considered offensive or inappropriate in another. Navigating this regulatory diversity demands a meticulous approach, involving legal expertise and constant monitoring of evolving legal landscapes in different markets.

Market Variations and Consumer Behavior

Every market is unique, shaped by its economic conditions, consumer behavior, and competition landscape. Digital marketing strategies that succeed in one market may not necessarily yield the same results elsewhere. Understanding local preferences, purchasing habits, and market trends is crucial for tailoring marketing campaigns effectively.

Consumer behavior can vary significantly, influencing the platforms and channels that are most effective for reaching target audiences. While social media platforms may dominate in some regions, others may favor search engines or local online forums. Adapting digital marketing strategies to align with these preferences requires continuous market research and a dynamic approach that can quickly respond to changing trends.

Technological Disparities and Accessibility

Globalization has not homogenized technological access. Disparities in internet infrastructure, device penetration, and digital literacy persist across different regions. In some areas, slow internet speeds and limited access to smartphones may impede the effectiveness of certain digital marketing tactics, such as video content or mobile apps.

Tailoring strategies to account for these technological variations is essential for reaching the widest possible audience. This may involve optimizing content for slower internet connections, designing mobile-friendly campaigns, or even considering alternative channels such as SMS marketing in regions with limited internet access.

The Rise of Social Media and Influencer Marketing

Social media has become a powerful force in the digital marketing landscape, providing a platform for global reach. However, the effectiveness of social media campaigns can vary significantly based on cultural preferences and local social media landscapes. While platforms like Facebook and Instagram are popular globally, specific networks dominate in different regions.

Moreover, the rise of influencer marketing introduces a new layer of complexity. Identifying influencers whose values align with the target audience requires a nuanced understanding of cultural norms. What may be considered authentic and relatable in one culture might not resonate with another. Building effective partnerships with influencers demands thorough research and an appreciation for cultural nuances.

Conclusion

In the dynamic landscape of digital marketing, globalization presents both opportunities and challenges. Adapting strategies for diverse audiences requires a multifaceted approach that addresses cultural sensitivities, linguistic nuances, regulatory landscapes, market variations, and technological disparities. The key to success lies in a deep understanding of the target audience and a commitment to tailoring digital marketing efforts to resonate with the unique characteristics of each market.

As businesses continue to expand globally, the ability to navigate these hurdles becomes increasingly vital. Embracing the diversity of the global marketplace and incorporating cultural intelligence into digital marketing strategies will not only enhance brand resonance but also foster lasting connections with audiences around the world. In the ever-evolving field of IT and digital marketing, overcoming the challenges of globalization is not just a necessity but a strategic imperative for sustained success.

Introduction

In the rapidly evolving landscape of IT and digital marketing, the demand for skilled professionals has reached unprecedented heights. The advent of new technologies, changing consumer behaviors, and the ever-expanding digital ecosystem have created a challenging yet dynamic environment. Companies are now engaged in what can be termed as "Digital Talent Wars", a fierce competition to acquire and retain the best minds in the field. This article delves into the challenges associated with finding and retaining skilled digital marketing professionals and explores strategies to bridge the widening skills gap.

The Shifting Landscape of Digital Marketing

The digital marketing landscape is in a constant state of flux. New technologies emerge, algorithms evolve, and consumer preferences change faster than ever before. As a result, the demand for professionals who can navigate this dynamic environment with finesse has skyrocketed. From data scientists and SEO specialists to content creators and social media managers, the digital marketing team must comprise a diverse skill set to stay ahead.

The Talent Crunch

One of the primary challenges in the digital talent wars is the scarcity of qualified professionals. The traditional education system struggles to keep pace with the rapid evolution of digital technologies. Consequently, there is a considerable gap between what is taught in classrooms and the practical skills demanded by the industry. Employers often find themselves sifting through a digital haystack, searching for the elusive needles – candidates with the right mix of skills and experience.

The Role of Specialized Skill Sets

Digital marketing is no longer a one-size-fits-all discipline. Different platforms, channels, and tools require specialized knowledge and skills. For instance, expertise in search engine optimization (SEO) does not necessarily translate into proficiency in social media management or data analytics. The challenge for businesses is not just to find skilled professionals but to assemble a team with a diverse skill set that covers the entire spectrum of digital marketing.

The Need for Continuous Learning and Adaptation

In the digital realm, stagnation is synonymous with obsolescence. Professionals must continuously update their skills to keep up with the latest trends and technologies. This poses a dual challenge for both employers and employees. Companies need to invest in training and development programs to ensure their workforce remains at the forefront of industry advancements. Simultaneously, professionals must embrace a mindset of lifelong learning to stay relevant in the ever-changing digital landscape.

The Competitive Job Market

The talent war doesn't end with recruitment; retaining skilled professionals is an equally daunting task. In a competitive job market, where every company is vying for top talent, retaining employees becomes a strategic imperative. The allure of better opportunities, more significant challenges, or superior work cultures often tempts skilled professionals to explore new horizons.

The Importance of Company Culture

Company culture plays a pivotal role in retaining digital marketing talent. Professionals in this field often seek environments that foster creativity, innovation, and a collaborative spirit. A workplace that encourages experimentation and provides a platform for employees to showcase their skills is more likely to retain top talent. Company culture is not just about ping-pong tables and casual Fridays; it's about creating an atmosphere where employees feel valued and motivated to contribute their best.

Career Growth and Advancement Opportunities

Digital marketing professionals are ambitious and driven by a desire for continuous career growth. Companies that offer clear paths for advancement and invest in the professional development of their employees are more likely to retain top talent. This involves not only providing training opportunities but also creating a structure that allows employees to take on new challenges and responsibilities as they progress in their careers.

Competitive Compensation and Benefits

While job satisfaction and a positive work environment are crucial, competitive compensation remains a significant factor in retaining skilled professionals. In the digital talent wars, companies must be willing to offer salaries and benefits that are not only competitive with industry standards but also reflective of the individual's skills and contributions. Employees who feel adequately compensated for their expertise are more likely to stay loyal to their current employer.

Flexible Work Arrangements and Work-Life Balance

Digital marketing often involves working on tight deadlines and adapting to real-time trends. In such a demanding environment, offering flexible work arrangements and promoting a healthy work-life balance can be a significant retention strategy. Companies that acknowledge the importance of employee well-being and provide the flexibility to manage work and personal commitments are more likely to retain their digital marketing talent.

Strategies to Bridge the Skills Gap

As the digital talent wars intensify, companies must adopt proactive strategies to bridge the skills gap and stay ahead in the competition.

1. Investment in Training and Development Programs

To address the shortage of qualified professionals, companies need to take the initiative in providing training and development programs. This can involve partnerships with educational institutions, online learning platforms, and in-house training initiatives. By nurturing talent from within, companies can build a skilled workforce that aligns with their specific needs.

2. Building Collaborative Ecosystems

The digital marketing landscape is vast and interconnected. Companies can bridge the skills gap by fostering collaborative ecosystems. This involves partnerships with other organizations, industry associations, and even competitors. By sharing knowledge and resources, companies can create a pool of shared expertise that benefits the entire ecosystem.

3. Embracing Diversity and Inclusion

A diverse team brings together a variety of perspectives and approaches, enhancing creativity and problem-solving. Companies should actively promote diversity and inclusion in their hiring practices. This not only helps in bridging the skills gap but also contributes to a more dynamic and innovative work environment.

4. Utilizing Freelancers and External Agencies

In the gig economy, many skilled professionals prefer the flexibility of freelance or contract work. Companies can leverage this trend by collaborating with freelancers or external agencies for specific projects or skill requirements. This not only provides access to specialized talent but also allows companies to adapt to changing needs without the long-term commitment of full-time hires.

5. Encouraging Continuous Learning

To keep up with the dynamic nature of digital marketing, companies should foster a culture of continuous learning. This involves providing employees with opportunities for skill enhancement, whether through workshops, online courses, or attending industry conferences. By encouraging a mindset of continuous improvement, companies can ensure that their workforce remains adaptable and up-to-date with the latest trends.

Conclusion

The digital talent wars in IT and digital marketing are a reflection of the rapid evolution of technology and consumer behavior. Bridging the skills gap requires a multifaceted approach that includes proactive recruitment, strategic retention efforts, and a commitment to continuous learning. In this era of digital transformation, companies that successfully navigate the talent wars will not only stay competitive but also drive innovation and shape the future of the digital landscape.

Introduction

In the ever-evolving landscape of digital marketing, organizations face a constant challenge: how to achieve maximum return on investment (ROI) while operating within budget constraints. As the digital realm expands and new platforms emerge, marketers find themselves under increasing pressure to demonstrate the effectiveness of their campaigns. This article delves into the intricacies of navigating the budget blues in digital marketing and explores strategies to optimize ROI.

The Shifting Paradigm of Digital Marketing

The digital marketing landscape has undergone a significant transformation in recent years, with emerging technologies, changing consumer behaviors, and evolving algorithms. As organizations strive to stay ahead, they often find their budgets stretched thin. The traditional channels of digital marketing, such as paid advertising and social media, are still essential, but diversification is key. Marketers must be adaptive, exploring new avenues like influencer marketing, content partnerships, and emerging platforms to make the most of their resources.

The Challenge of Attribution Models

One of the primary hurdles in maximizing ROI is the difficulty in accurately attributing conversions to specific digital marketing efforts. The customer journey is multifaceted, involving various touchpoints across different channels. As a result, determining which aspects of a campaign contribute most significantly to conversions becomes a complex puzzle. Marketers grapple with the challenge of establishing reliable attribution models that provide a holistic view of the customer journey, enabling them to allocate resources effectively.

Data-Driven Decision Making

In the quest for optimal ROI, organizations must harness the power of data-driven decision-making. Analyzing data provides valuable insights into consumer behavior, preferences, and the performance of different marketing channels. By leveraging analytics tools, marketers can identify high-performing strategies and reallocate budgets accordingly. A data-driven approach enables organizations to trim the fat from less effective channels, maximizing the impact of their digital marketing spend.

Content is King

In the digital age, content remains a cornerstone of successful marketing strategies. However, the emphasis has shifted from sheer volume to quality. Marketers face the challenge of producing content that not only captivates their audience but also aligns with search engine algorithms. Investing in high-quality, engaging content pays dividends in terms of organic reach and audience engagement. This approach, although potentially requiring a higher initial investment, ensures sustained ROI over time.

Social Media Strategies on a Shoestring Budget

A *"shoestring budget"* refers to a minimal or extremely tight budget, typically with very limited financial resources. It implies that an individual or organization is operating with the bare minimum funds necessary to carry out their activities, often requiring frugality and careful financial management.

Social media platforms are integral to digital marketing, providing a direct line of communication with target audiences. However, maintaining a robust social media presence can strain budgets, especially for smaller businesses. Marketers must employ savvy strategies to maximize ROI on social media. This includes leveraging user-generated content, engaging with followers authentically, and strategically utilizing paid advertising to reach specific demographics. A careful balance between organic and paid strategies can yield significant returns without breaking the bank.

The Rise of Influencer Marketing

In the era of ad-blockers and banner blindness, influencer marketing has emerged as a powerful tool for reaching consumers. Partnering with influencers allows organizations to tap into established, engaged audiences without the hefty costs associated with traditional advertising. However, navigating the influencer landscape requires careful consideration of authenticity, relevance, and alignment with brand values. Marketers must strike a balance between budgetary constraints and the potential for impactful influencer collaborations.

SEO: A Long-Term Investment

Search engine optimization (SEO) is a cornerstone of digital marketing that offers long-term benefits. While achieving a high ranking on search engine results pages (SERPs) may take time, the sustained visibility and organic traffic it generates can significantly boost ROI. Marketers must view SEO as a long-term investment, allocating resources to optimize website content, improve site speed, and build quality backlinks. A well-executed SEO strategy ensures that organizations continue to reap rewards over an extended period, making it a cost-effective approach in the long run.

Leveraging Automation for Efficiency

Budget constraints often lead to resource limitations, making efficiency a crucial consideration in digital marketing efforts. Automation tools can streamline repetitive tasks, allowing marketers to focus on strategy and creativity. From email marketing to social media scheduling, automation not only saves time but also enhances consistency and precision in campaign execution. By investing in the right automation tools, organizations can stretch their budgets further and achieve a higher ROI.

A/B Testing: Refining Strategies for Success

A/B testing, also known as split testing, is a method used in marketing and product development to compare two versions of a webpage, email, app, or other content to determine which one performs better. In an A/B test, two variants (A and B) are compared by presenting them to similar audiences randomly. The goal is to identify which variant yields better results in terms of user engagement, conversions, or other key performance indicators. This helps businesses make data-driven decisions and optimize their content or features based on real user responses.

In the dynamic landscape of digital marketing, what works today may not yield the same results tomorrow. A/B testing is a valuable tool for refining strategies and maximizing ROI. By systematically testing different elements of campaigns - such as ad copy, visuals, and calls to action - marketers can identify the most effective variations. This iterative process enables organizations to optimize their digital marketing efforts continuously, ensuring that budgetary allocations align with the strategies delivering the best results.

The Importance of Customer Retention

While acquiring new customers is vital, retaining existing ones is equally - if not more - important for maximizing ROI. Repeat customers often require less marketing spend, making them a cost-effective source of revenue. Digital marketing strategies should include initiatives aimed at customer retention, such as personalized email campaigns, loyalty programs, and exclusive offers. By nurturing existing relationships, organizations can create a loyal customer base that contributes significantly to long-term ROI.

Conclusion

Navigating the budget blues in digital marketing requires a strategic and adaptive approach. Organizations must embrace the evolving landscape, diversify their efforts, and leverage data-driven insights to make informed decisions. By prioritizing quality content, exploring cost-effective social media strategies, and embracing long-term investments like SEO, marketers can maximize ROI within budget constraints. Influencer marketing, automation, A/B testing, and a focus on customer retention further contribute to a holistic and effective digital marketing strategy. In the face of challenges, organizations that innovate and optimize their approach will find themselves not only weathering the budget blues but also achieving sustainable success in the dynamic realm of digital marketing.

As we embark on the final chapter of our exploration into the multifaceted world of "*Challenges in IT and Digital Marketing*", it is apt to take a moment to reflect on the journey we've traversed. From the ever-changing technological landscape to the intricacies of compliance and the omnipresent threat of cyber-attacks, each chapter has unraveled a layer of complexity that defines the contemporary terrain of IT and digital marketing.

Adaptation as the Cornerstone

In the opening chapter, we delved into the relentless pace of technological evolution. The narrative emphasized the imperative for organizations to embrace adaptability as a cornerstone for survival. As we stand on the precipice of the future, this ability to adapt becomes even more critical. The pace of change shows no sign of abating, and those who thrive will be the ones who can pivot swiftly, transforming challenges into opportunities.

Continuous Learning

Chapter 2 shed light on the importance of continuous learning in IT. The half-life of skills is diminishing rapidly, making perpetual learning a professional mandate. The future belongs to those who see education not as a phase but as a constant, evolving companion. The digital professional of tomorrow must be a perpetual student, ever-curious and eager to acquire new skills to stay relevant.

Leadership in the Digital Era

Leadership emerged as a recurrent theme in our exploration. Whether aligning IT with business goals or steering organizations through the tumultuous waters of compliance and cybersecurity, effective leadership has been the linchpin. As we look to the future, the role of leaders becomes even more pivotal. Visionaries who can navigate uncertainty, inspire innovation, and foster collaboration will be the architects of success in the digital age.

Ethics in the Digital Realm

The third chapter spotlighted the guardianship of the digital realm. Cybersecurity, a perpetual cat-and-mouse game, necessitates ethical considerations. The digital landscape is not just a playground for innovation; it's a realm where ethical choices carry profound consequences. As technology continues to intertwine with every aspect of our lives, the ethical dimensions of digital decisions will define the integrity of businesses and their leaders.

Collaboration and Communication

Chapters 5 and 6 explored the challenges posed by interdepartmental jargon and the imperative of aligning IT with business goals. Bridging the communication gap and fostering collaboration between IT and other departments emerged as strategic imperatives. As we gaze into the future, breaking down silos and nurturing cross-functional collaboration will be essential for organizations to thrive in the digital landscape.

Strategies for Success in Project Management

Chapters 7 and 8 navigated the rocky terrains of scope creep, project pains, and tight timelines. Successful project management strategies were revealed to be a delicate blend of foresight, adaptability, and effective communication. Looking forward, organizations must hone these skills to face the challenges of an increasingly interconnected and time-sensitive world.

Digital Marketing in the Algorithmic Age

Shifting our focus to digital marketing in Chapters 9 to 16, we explored algorithmic adventures, data privacy dilemmas, content overload, real-time engagement, decoding digital data, globalization hurdles, talent wars, and budget blues. In this symphony of challenges, one resounding note emerged – the human element. Behind every data point, algorithm, or marketing strategy, there is a human being. As we steer into the future, successful digital marketing will be anchored in authentic, human-centric experiences.

The Human Element, Diversity, and Inclusion

Diversity and inclusion, often touched upon in our exploration, now take center stage. The narrative of the future is incomplete without addressing the imperative of a diverse workforce and inclusive practices. The digital revolution must be a force for societal good, breaking down barriers rather than fortifying them.

Resilience as the North Star

In a business context, the term "North Star" is often used to refer to a central, guiding metric or objective that helps align the efforts and goals of a team or organization. The North Star metric is a key performance indicator (KPI) that is considered essential for the success and growth of the business. It serves as a focal point, guiding strategic decisions and actions to ensure that all efforts contribute toward achieving that central objective. The concept is derived from navigation, where the North Star has historically been used as a reliable point of reference for determining direction.

As we conclude this journey, it is essential to advocate for resilience as the North Star guiding our endeavors. Resilience is not just the ability to bounce back from adversity; it's the capacity to transform challenges into catalysts for growth. In the unpredictable landscape of IT and digital marketing, resilience is the difference between surviving and thriving.

Industry Trends, Predictions, and an Optimistic Outlook

Peering into the crystal ball, what can we discern about the future of IT and digital marketing? Industry trends indicate a deeper integration of AI and machine learning, an increased emphasis on sustainability, and a growing reliance on data analytics. Organizations that can harness these trends while staying true to ethical principles will emerge as leaders.

Predictions aside, our outlook is inherently optimistic. Challenges are not roadblocks but stepping stones to progress. The dynamic landscapes of IT and digital marketing are not adversaries but canvases waiting for the strokes of innovation. The future belongs to those who dare to dream, adapt, collaborate, and above all, embrace the human element in the digital revolution.

In the closing words of this chapter and the broader book, let us embark on the future with open minds, resilient spirits, and a commitment to continuous learning. The challenges are formidable, but so is our capacity to overcome them. The future of IT and digital marketing is not just a destination; it's a journey we navigate together, leveraging our collective strengths to shape a landscape where technology serves humanity, and digital marketing resonates authentically with diverse audiences.

"Challenges in IT and Digital Marketing" is an insightful exploration of the rapidly evolving landscapes of technology and marketing in the digital age. In this comprehensive volume, the book delves into the multifaceted hurdles faced by IT professionals and digital marketers alike, addressing critical issues that shape the industry. From the breakneck pace of technological change to the perpetual battle against cyber threats, each chapter examines a distinct challenge. Topics range from the intricacies of regulatory compliance and communication gaps between technical and non-technical stakeholders to the pressures of tight project timelines and the constant quest for real-time engagement in the digital marketing sphere.

With a keen eye on the future, the book also explores the ongoing challenges of talent acquisition and retention in the dynamic digital marketplace. Whether you are an IT professional seeking to navigate the ever-changing tech terrain or a digital marketer aiming to maximize ROI in a budget-conscious environment, this book provides valuable insights and strategies to overcome the hurdles and thrive in the challenging realms of IT and digital marketing.

ABOUT THE AUTHOR

Mr. C. P. Kumar is a retired Scientist 'G' from National Institute of Hydrology, Roorkee, Uttarakhand, India. He is also a Reiki Healer and Chakra Balancing practitioner (with pendulum dowsing) and offers Emotional Freedom Technique (EFT) to help individuals with emotional issues. Mr. Kumar has authored many books on technical, spiritual, and social topics.

For further details, you may visit his webpage
https://www.angelfire.com/nh/cpkumar/virgo.html